# SCRAM!

Written by Anthony Robinson

Illustrated by Betty Edwards

Scrump and Strack were friends.
They had lots of fun!

They crept into the sandpit.
Strack got a sock.

Strack and Scrump ran.

The friends ran.
They ran in a zigzag.

Scrump jumped into the pond.

Quack! Quack!

Strack fell into the pond!

7

"Quick," said Scrump. "Sprint!"

Scrump and Strack ran
into a picnic.
The pop was spilt.

q

"Quick," said Strack. "Sprint!"
The friends ran and ran.

Yuck!

They ran into the mud.
It went splat!